Drop-shipping

How to make $1000 Per Day Passive Income Online with eBay Dropshipping

Table of Contents

Introduction

I want to thank you and congratulate you for downloading the book, "Dropshipping - How to make $1000 Per Day Passive Income Online with eBay Dropshipping".

This book contains proven steps and strategies on how to build a 5(and even 6!)-figure drop shipping empire on eBay. With this information, you will be able to make passive income while working on your job, or quit you job and travel the world.

This is a location independent business and for those who are willing to commit, it pays big dividends. I was able to quit my job and enjoy a life of abundance thanks to this method. This is not a regular drop-shipping tutorial – In this book, I will teach you how to crash your competition, make more money per sale, and bring something else to the table, that will make eBay love you and drive more traffic to your listings. All you need to do is take items from other websites and list them on ebay!

I know, I know. Sounds too good to be true. Perhaps too easy. At the beginning, I thought so too – but I committed to it, and was able to make 5-figures income. I hired a virtual assistant to help me manage my store, and now I don't have to work more than 30 minutes a day. This business model is amazing. Here is a screenshot of my ebay account:

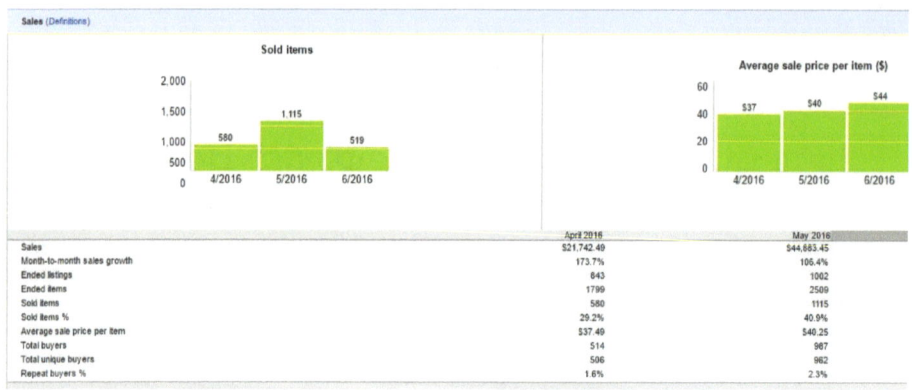

	April 2016	May 2016
Sales	$21,742.49	$44,885.45
Month-to-month sales growth	173.7%	106.4%
Ended listings	843	1002
Ended items	1799	2509
Sold items	580	1115
Sold items %	29.2%	40.9%
Average sale price per item	$37.49	$40.25
Total buyers	514	967
Total unique buyers	506	962
Repeat buyers %	1.6%	2.3%

Now, let's make some money.

Chapter 1 – What is a Drop Shipping Business?

Before I get into the exact definition, I want you to understand something very important: - There are different forms and different techniques to drop shipping. What I'm going to teach you, is one form of drop shipping called "retail arbitrage", or e-drop shipping. But first, let's dive into the definition of drop shipping:

According to Wikipedia, drop shipping is a supply chain management technique in which the **retailer does not keep goods** in stock, but instead **transfers customer orders** and shipment details to either the manufacturer or a wholesaler, who then ships the goods directly to the customer.

What you're going to learn, is a similar technique, however, more efficient, cleverer, with a higher profit potential. Instead of using "a supplier" we will use "a source".

So what's a source?

A source can be any website that sells goods online. It can be amazon.com, homedepot.com, walmart.com and – funny enough – even ebay.com.

What we are going to do, is simply copy & paste:

We will take products from our source, copy their images, description, details, and list them on eBay.

For example, we can take a $100 tool box on homedepot.com, and list it on eBay for $150. When someone buys our product, the money goes to our Paypal account, and we will take our $150, go on homedepot.com, add this item to our cart, fill in the customer's shipping address, and pay $100. After eBay fees, PayPal fees, and sales tax, we will gain about $25 in profit. Not bad for only one buyer out of the hundred million buyers on eBay.

Chapter 2 – Set Your Seller Account

On ebay.com, click on register.

Fill in your email address, preferred password and the rest.

Now you have an eBay account – However, not optimized for selling.

On the left top corner, you should see a text saying "Hi [your_name]!". Hover on that text, and you should have a link for "account settings".

In the middle of the screen, you can see an article titled " How to sell items on eBay". On that article, click on the link saying "Learn more":

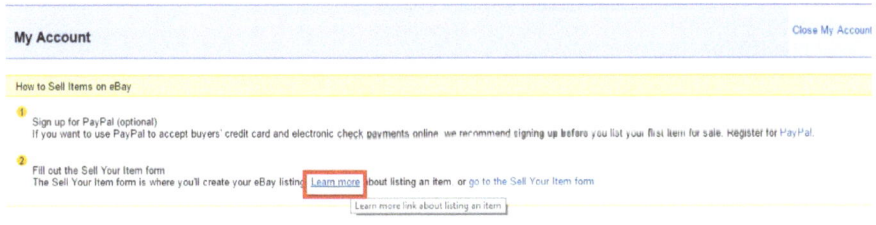

From there, you'll want to click on "Getting started selling on eBay" under the related topics window on the right side.

In the middle of the screen, click on the "Set up a seller account" link.

1. Set up a seller account

- Confirm that the name and address we have on file for you is correct
- Confirm your phone number
- Specify an automatic payment method for paying your seller fees and eBay Money Back Guarantee reimbursements
- We also recommend that you get PayPal Verified

Set up a seller account

Have your credit card ready and your phone next to you. I trust you to go from here by yourself – Simply, fill in your country, phone number, addresses and anything else eBay asks you to provide. EBay will text you or call you to confirm you are a real person, so cooperate with them. You'll thank me later.

One thing you should have in mind – at some point, eBay will ask how you would like to pay your fees. Fees will be explained later in the book – for now, choose the most convenient way for you to pay fees (You pay nothing until you sell so no risk is involved). You can choose PayPal, credit card or even a bank withdrawal.

The second account you'll need is a PayPal account. Setting a PayPal account is more simple. Just go to Paypal.com and fill in the information they ask you to provide.

You must open a PayPal account in your own country, use your true name, true bank account, true age. Trust me, be honest with PayPal. You don't want to get your account limited. You also have to option to start a PayPal business account – I recommend you to start a regular account and upgrade later, when your business is more solid.

Once you set an eBay account and a PayPal account, you are ready to go!

Chapter 3– Optimizing Your Account for Selling on eBay

We can have slight advantage over other sellers by optimizing our account and make eBay like us with our selling preferences. However, I'm not going to go in details on why you should set X preference like this or the other way, but instead, I will go straight to the point and tell you what to type and choose. You will understand by common sense why you should set your account like that, but if you are still curious, go on google.com and find the answer!

On account settings, click on "Site Preferences".

Selling Preferences

Use the out of stock option -> Yes

Payment from buyers

[Check V] Offer PayPal on my listings -> Offer Paypal as a payment method in all my listings

[Check V] Tell Buyers that I prefer PayPal payments

[Check V] Include my items when buyers pay all their sellers at once using PayPal

Shipping Preferences

Offer the Global Shipping Program -> Yes (At this point, you'll be redirected to a new window where eBay will explain what is GSP. The book will also touch this subject later)

Exclude shipping locations -> Exclude Alaska/Hawaii, US Protectorates, APO/FPO.

Unpaid Item Assistant

Let eBay open and close unpaid item cases for you automatically -> Check 'Yes'

Open a case if payment hasn't been received after -> 4 days

EBay Username

My eBay -> Selling -> Account(Tab) -> Personal Information

EBay username does not really affect how well you will be doing. However, it's a 1% of advantage if you have a nice username. Choose a username like 'bestdeals2017', 'bestmoneysavers' or any other "cheesy" username that will determine that you are here to sell, you aren't a dabbler. As long as you don't choose "Hotgirls456" or something like that, you are good to go.

Chapter 4 – Choosing Products to Sell

Obviously, we need some items in our eBay store in order to make a profit.

Now the question is – What items should I sell? What category? What price range?

And the answer is – Everything, and anything. Yes. I mean that.

You don't want to get so caught up in what items will sell. Listing items on eBay is free (to a certain degree). We need to take advantage of that, and also, look at this from a productive point of view.

Let's say we need to spend about 20 minutes to find a hot item to sell. In 20 minutes, we can list at least 4 items! And even if you do spend some time on market research, nothing will guarantee that your item will sell, so you have a better chance selling something by listing 4 random items than 1 "might-be-hot" item in 20 minutes.

This approach is the most productive approach to this kind of business. Just list everything and see what sticks. Of course, you can add some intelligence to it – If it's summer, you can try selling pool inflatables. If it's Christmas, you can sell decorative lights, or even log racks. The key is – Don't overthink it. This is a numbers game, the bigger the store, the bigger the paycheck, just be consistent and list as many items as you can.

Chapter 5 - Crush Your Competition

If you still don't believe the best method for selling on ebay is listing everything and anything, here is my way to find hot items on eBay.

Randomly, pick an item from your source. For this example, we will take this item from homedepot.com:http://www.homedepot.com/p/Rub bermaid-Roughneck-32-Gal-Recycling-Bin-1792641/202260842

We will copy the model number of this item (1792641) and make a search for it on eBay:

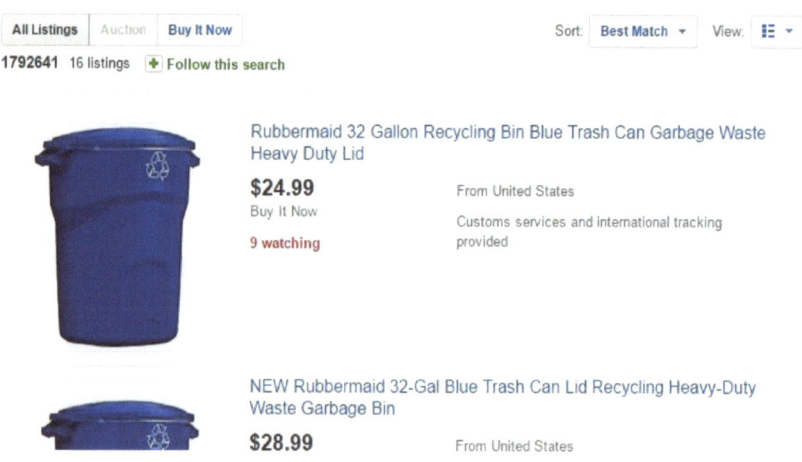

As you can see, eBay found 16 listings using that model number. That means we have just found 16 competitors. Obviously, they are drop shippers as well – they have the same pictures, model numbers and the descriptions are identical to those on homedepot.com. We want to compete only with other drop shippers – people who sell physical products from their house/warehouse are out of the game.

After clicking on the first listing, I can see that this seller has sold this item 6 times. By clicking on the "6 sold" link, I can see he sold 6 of them in the last 30 days. As a rule of thumb, items that were sold more than 4 times in the last 30 days are considered best sellers.

We found a winner. We are going to sell this item as well.

You also want to build a list of competitors, like the 16 competitors I found, and follow them. Track every hot items they have and sell it as well. Don't make it easy on them – Dominate the market.

Chapter 6 – Hacking SEO on eBay

In order to sell a lot, we need to focus on 1 thing, and one thing only:

Get on the first page of the search results on eBay.

Before I teach you how to optimize your listings and everything else so eBay will rank you higher in the "Best Match" search results, I want you to understand – eBay is rewarding good sellers. Ebay looks for sellers who provide a great buying experience. Of course – using great titles and great pictures on your listings will help you, and we will get to that in the next chapter, but in order to really crush it on ebay you will have to gain some great seller history, provide superb customer service to your buyers, never leave a customer angry.

EBay search results algorithm, also known as Cassini, will give you a general seller score depends on various things. The variations below will give you a better understanding of how Cassini works:

- Item Is New vs. Used

- Top Seller Status (Below standard, Above standard or Top Seller)

- Auctions vs. Fixed Price (Hint: most of the sales on eBay are on fixed price listings)

- Seller's defect rate (Constantly changing – As for now, a seller defect is either a cancelled transaction because seller went out of stock or a buyer opens a case against a seller)

- Buyer locations & Seller location

- Feedback score & amount

- Buyer's patterns on eBay

- Price

- Hassle-free returns

- Length of return window

- Global shipping offered on listings

- Shipping cost vs. Free shipping

- Number of photos – More photos, Higher ranking

- Quality of photos – Good photos (Size & quality), Higher ranking

- Handling time – Shorter handling time (The time it takes you to ship the item after you get a sale), better ranking

- Seller's total number of listed items – More items, better ranking

- Seller's total number of listed items on a specific category – More items in a specific category, Better ranking in a specific category

- Detailed Seller Rank (DSR – How buyers rank you in details when they leave a feedback)

- Cases opened

- Seller's return rate – The more returns you have, the lower eBay will rank you in the search results

- Newly listed – New listings get a temporary boost

- Ending soon – Listings that are about to end get a temporarily boost

- Impressions – The more impressions you get without an action by the buyer (The more times your listings are shown on the search results and buyers skip it/don't take any action) – The lower eBay will rank your listing in the search resultes

- Shopping device

- Category

- Clicks

- Views - Like impressions, if you get a lot of views without any action by the buyer (Could be adding to watch list, messaging the seller and of course purchasing the item), eBay will push you down in the search results.

- Fast & Free shipping

- Repeat buyer rate for sellers

- Tracking uploaded

- How long you've been a seller

As you can see, eBay is looking at the overall picture of a seller. The lowest price is not enough. EBay wants their buyers to enjoy the whole process of purchasing on their website. Optimize all of the above – and you will achieve extraordinary results.

Also understand - each buyer gets a different search results. You can't rank all of your items at the first place on the search results all the time.

Chapter 7 – Optimize your listings and rank #1

Fill in the blank:

The most important thing on selling on ebay is:

_____

If you didn't answer getting on the first page of the search results, you need to go back to the previous chapter.

Even though eBay looks at the overall picture of a seller, we can still have a search results boost by optimizing our listings.

We will optimize our listings using **keywords** in our title, providing as many **item identifiers** as we can, and using as many **pictures** as we can.

Let's say we want to sell a tool box. I use homedepot.com a lot since it's not saturated like amazon.com, and I know that tool boxes are sold in a high volume on eBay. Here is how to list an item & optimize it to eBay search engine (aka Cassini):

Category

First of all, we need to choose the right category. This is a big factor. In the search form, simply type what you're selling. Usually, the first result will be the best category to choose, but sometimes you need to think like a buyer and ask yourself: "If I wanted to buy 'X' on eBay, what category will I choose to find it?"

TITLE

When writing the title, we want to use as many keywords as we can. If the title on Home Depot is "52-inch Metal Tool Box", we want to change, add or remove words in order to make it "user friendly" on eBay. I usually use title-builder.com. Type in 1-2 words what you're selling on title-builder.com and it will generate keywords for that item. We have 80 characters to use for our title, and we want to use them all. An optimized title will look like:

"Stanely 52 in. Tool Box Chest Cabinet, Toolbox Storage Rolling New"

PHOTOS

Download all the pictures and images from your source to your computer, and upload them to your listing. EBay loves listings with a lot of pictures, and it will boost you on the search results. You can also upload the same picture multiple times.

ITEM SPECIFICS

Each category requires different item specifics, such as brand, voltage, color, etc. You want to fill **all of them.** Don't leave any field empty. Even if you don't know the item's model number, just type something, or choose "Does Not Apply". When you leave some fields empty, eBay's search engine will rank you lower in the search results since the listing is incomplete.

Also, by filling all of the fields, you give the chance to users to find the item they are looking for.

DESCRIPTION

Simply copy the exact same description from your source and paste it into your listing. Try to delete any HTML code and use 1 color (preferably black). Delete any unnecessary sentences such as "only available at Home Depot!" or "If you have any questions call 1-800-900-900".

PRICE

As a rule of thumb, I multiply the original price at my source by 1.5. So if an item costs $100, I will price it on eBay for $150. You can play with it and see what works for you. Pay attention, you will be charged around 10% of the sales price by eBay as final value fee, about 3% of the sale price will be paid for PayPal fee, and the source(maybe) will charge you around 7% sales tax. Just pay attention you don't lose any money for selling your item.

At first, listing an item will take you a lot of time, but similar to everything else in the world, practice it and you will do it better & faster. Remember, the bigger the store the bigger the paycheck, so don't stop after 1 item – list as many as possible!

Chapter 8 – Processing Orders

Once you get a sale, you will get an email + eBay notification. In this notification, you'll see the buyer's information, and the item he bought. When I need to process my orders, I simply go to My eBay -> Selling -> Awaiting shipment. It looks like this:

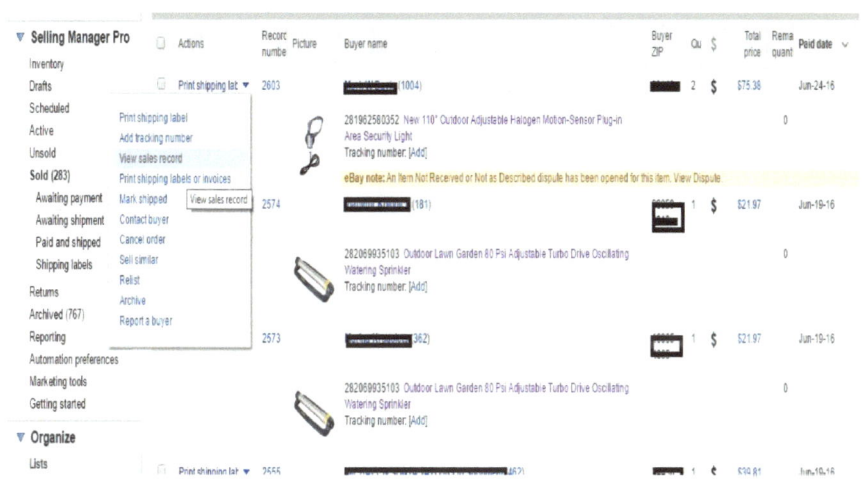

After clicking on sale's record, I can see my buyer's address and contact information.

Now, go to your source, add the exact same item to your cart, and click checkout. In my case, you can see that I sold 2 lights, so I will go to homedepot.com, and add those 2 items to my cart.

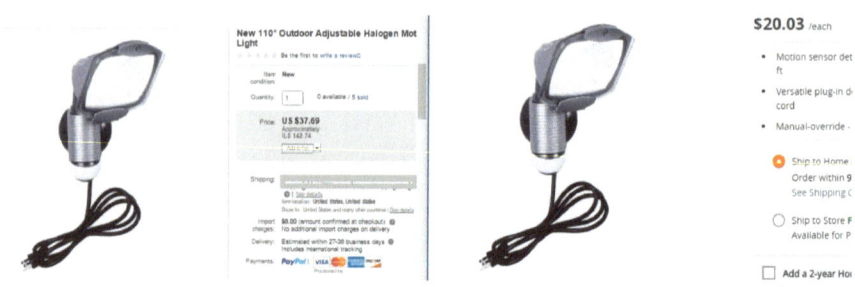

As you can see, they are sold for $20 on Home Depot, and I sold them for $37. After fees, I made around $25 just from this single sale!

Your source will ask you for your shipping address – this is where you copy & paste your buyer's shipping address (you can find it by clicking 'order details' on

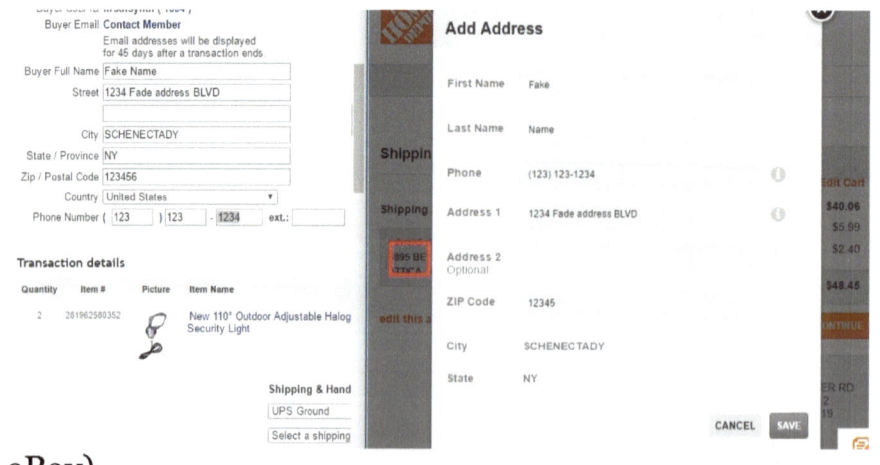

eBay).

Now, all you need to do is to pay, and you'll be redirected to an order confirmation page. Make sure the shipping address matches your buyer's shipping address, and your workday is over. Home Depot will ship it to your customer while you can have a margarita on the beach.

Chapter 9 – Uploading Tracking Numbers

Your source will provide a tracking number for the package around 1-3 business days after you made the purchase. You will get a shipping confirmation email with the details and the tracking number. All you need to do is copy that tracking number and add it to your order details on eBay. That way, eBay will track that you're a fast shipper and give you a better seller score – which makes you rank higher in the search results. Your customer will be happy to follow the package as well.

Chapter 12 – What Sources to Use

Amazon.com

Pros: Millions of products, fast shipping. Great customer service, super easy return process.

Cons: Having the prime membership is helpful. Do not abuse the membership (=use it too often) or Amazon will ban you.

I don't use Amazon since it's over-saturated in my opinion. I use them sometimes when my original source is out of stock.

Bedbathbeyond.com

Pros: Cool source, few hundred thousand products. You can use PayPal directly if you are outside of USA, versus similar sources that will not accept payments from a foreign PayPal account. They also have some unique items that are hard to get in other places.

Cons: A little too expensive.

I use them to find items that are not sold on other websites.

Walmart.com

Pros: Great source, few hundred thousand products. Fast shipping, Easy to use, often offers the best price.

Cons: A little too saturated, this source became pretty popular among drop-shippers.

Homedepot.com

Pros: My favorite source. Way less competitive, offers free shipping on most items over $49. Lots of exclusive brands, easy to contact customer service via chat.

Cons: Returns are little messy.

lowes.com

Pros: My second favorite source, way less competitive. Lots of exclusive brands only to Lowes.

Cons: Shipping time is sometimes delayed (but most of the times – super fast shipping)

My last piece of advice to you – the sky is the limit. There are hundreds of sources and websites you can use, including Chinese websites like aliexpress.com or Alibaba.com. It's your business – You need to decide how it will look like. The beautiful thing about this business model, is that you will always have something different to list, something new to sell, and the options are endless.

Chapter 10 – Increase Your Profits by Using Cashback Websites

I use topcashback.com for every purchase I make online. I get around 5% cashback, which generates me additional $1500 profit every month! Don't leave money on the table, before you process your orders, login into topcashback.com, find your source's website, and get cashback for your purchase. You want to do that from your very first sale. You can use any cashback website you want.

Chapter 11 – Increasing your selling limits

Every seller on eBay has some form of a limitation on his/her account.

EBay value their buyers above all else – and for a good reason. Without the buyers, eBay cannot exist, and like we learned previously in the book, the buying experience is vital for success on eBay.

Therefore, they are limiting the amount of sales & the amount of listings each user can make a month – Just to protect themselves from scammers and frauds.

Every single month, you will have to call eBay and discuss about your limits with a representative from eBay. Before you call, make sure you are very close to your monthly limits (list all the listings you can list) – Sometimes eBay will not increase your limits just because you are not even close to your ceiling. You can also contact them by email – however, eBay want you to call them to make sure you are a real legit person.

EBay will ask you what do you sell, where are you getting your items from, what type of products do you usually sell, where do you live, etc. Answer their questions with complete honesty and eBay will be happy to raise your limits.

Sometimes drop shippers are trying to hide the fact that they are drop shipping. This will only make things worse. EBay knows what drop shipping is, and in fact, they are encouraging people to drop ship on their website! Be proud to tell them that you are a drop shipper!

Chapter 11 – Reducing PayPal fees

For every sale you'll make, PayPal will take a nice cut of 2.9%+30c. If you make a sale from a user which has a foreign PayPal account, your fees will jump to 3.4%+30c. Although that sounds a little, in this kind of business, with that low profit margins, that will hurt our pocket.

The good news is – you can get a fees discount and reduce them up to 1.9%+30c per sale!

Purchase payments received (monthly)	Fee per transaction
$0.00 USD - $3,000.00 USD	2.9% + $0.30 USD
$3,000.01 USD - $10,000.00 USD	2.5% + $0.30 USD
$10,000.01 USD - $100,000.00 USD	2.2% + $0.30 USD
> $100,000.00 USD	1.9% + $0.30 USD†

†Does not apply to Website Payments Pro or Virtual Terminal.

PayPal Fees Table

As soon as you make more than $3000 in sales (not even in profit – in sales!), you'll want to call PayPal and ask for a fees discount. You just need to call them once and then they will adjust the fees discount automatically, according to your monthly revenue.

Chapter 11 – How Drop-Shipping Really Changes Lives

After listing 500 items in my store, I realized this job takes too much time of my day. And this is where the magic started.

I went to upwork.com and hired my first(ever!) virtual assistant. I taught him how to upload listings, how to upload tracking numbers, process orders – almost everything I know. Now, I hire 2 virtual assistants, and both of them work for me with a true loyalty. This leaves me to check emails once a day, for 30 minutes, and do what I love. I spend my days learning new business models, practice my guitar, and – believe it or not – I spend 3 days of the week getting tan on the beach. My VA's work for me, and the best part – It costs me $300 to get their really great services on my side.

More than that – I can now fly anywhere in the world for free. I enrolled an American Express program in which every dollar I spend; I get a mile to fly. With drop shipping, I spend more than $20,000 a month, which converts to miles and other benefits I can use. Life never seemed so good – Thinking 2 years backwards, I was desperate for money, and worked as a waiter in a restaurant I hated. Now, the future never seemed so bright. And you can have it too. All you have to do is EXECUTE , Focus on listing more items, practice eBay, become the best you can. There is enough money for everybody on eBay – just get your share of the pie.

Conclusion

Thank you again for downloading this book!

I hope this book was able to help you to achieve financial freedom.

The next step is to EXECUTE. List EVERYTHING and ANYTHING. Call eBay and ask them to raise your seller limits. Remember, the bigger the store, the bigger the paycheck – the more you list the more you earn. Don't quit after 1, 10 or even 100 listings – Keep on listing and you'll get extraordinary results.

Finally, if you enjoyed this book, then I'd like to ask you for a HUGE favor, would you be kind enough to leave a review for this book on Amazon? It'd be greatly appreciated!

Thank you and good luck!